HAL LEONARD

SNARE DRUM METHOD

THE MUSICAL APPROACH TO SNARE DRUM FOR BAND AND ORCHESTRA

BY RICK MATTINGLY

ISBN 0-634-03642-4

HAL•LEONARD®
CORPORATION

7777 W. BLUEMOUND RD. P.O. BOX 13819 MILWAUKEE, WI 53213

In Australia Contact:
Hal Leonard Australia Pty. Ltd.
22 Taunton Drive P.O. Box 5130
Cheltenham East, 3192 Victoria, Australia
Email: ausadmin@halleonard.com

Visit Hal Leonard Online at
www.halleonard.com

CONTENTS

CD TRACKS

Snare Drum recorded at Falk Studios, Louisville, KY

Snare Drum: Brian Kushmaul

Engineer: Tim Haertel

HOLDING THE STICKS

Matched Grip

Matched grip gets its name from the fact that both sticks are held the same way. Almost all drummers now use matched grip, whether they play snare drum in school band or orchestra, parade drum in marching band or drum corps, or drumset.

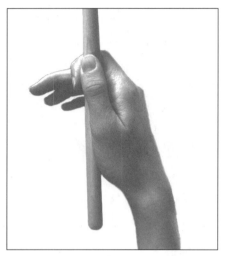

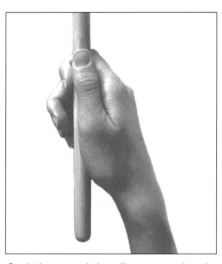

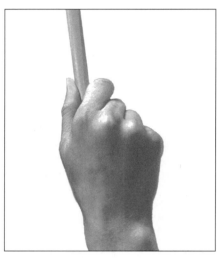

Start by grasping the stick between the thumb and first finger about two-thirds of the distance between the tip of the stick and the butt end.

Curl the remaining fingers under the stick, but do not press them tightly against the stick. Keep the hand relaxed.

The stick and the forearm should form a straight line.

The top of the drum should be positioned so that the forearms are angled down very slightly between the elbow and the wrist. The sticks should form about a 45 to 90 degree angle.

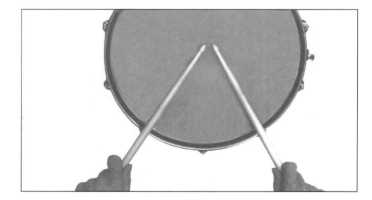

The elbows should be beside the body; they should not stick out behind your back, nor should you reach way out in front of your body to strike the drum.

Correct

Drum too close to body

Drum too far from body

Traditional Grip

Traditional grip was developed in order to accommodate a drum that was tilted as a result of being attached to a sling that was worn over the shoulder. Therefore, if you are using traditional grip, the drum should be titled slightly. The right hand grips the stick the same way in traditional grip as it does in matched grip.

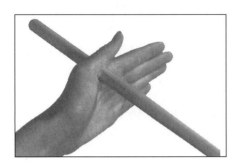

For the left-hand grip, start by holding the hand straight out with the wrist perpendicular to the floor. Insert the stick into the crevice between the thumb and palm.

Curl the little finger and ring finger under the stick, so that the stick rests on the middle joint of the ring finger.

Now curl the first and middle fingers over the stick, but do not let them touch it. The stick is held between the thumb and hand, not between the fingers. The ring finger supports the weight of the stick when it is at rest. The first finger helps push the stick down when making a downstroke.

MAKING THE STROKE

Matched Grip — Both Hands

Concentrate on the wrist when making a stroke. Start with the stick several inches above the drum. (The louder the note, the higher the stick should be before beginning the stroke.) With a quick, snapping motion of the wrist, bring the stick down. Keep the wrist relaxed so that as soon as the stick strikes the drumhead it can rebound off of it, as though the tip of the stick is a basketball that you are dribbling. Let the stick return to its starting position. The idea is for the stick to make the drumhead vibrate, not for the stick to have a collision with the drum!

Traditional Grip — Left Hand

To make the left-hand stroke with traditional grip, keep the wrist and forearm in a straight line, and twist the forearm quickly toward the drum, much like the motion you would use to turn a doorknob. The instant the stick hits the drumhead, let it rebound off the head and return to its starting position.

THE SNARE DRUM

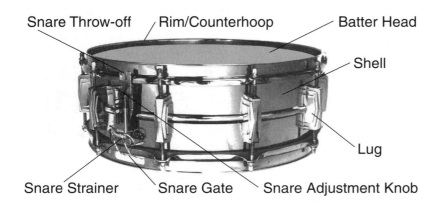

Snare Throw-off   Rim/Counterhoop   Batter Head
Shell
Lug
Snare Strainer   Snare Gate   Snare Adjustment Knob

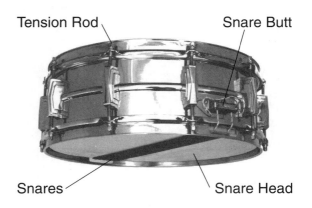

Tension Rod   Snare Butt
Snares   Snare Head

PRACTICE PADS

Most drummers have a practice pad, which enables them to practice snare drum without generating all of the volume that a drum produces. Also, it is easier to carry a practice pad back and forth between home and school than it is to carry a drum.

There are several different types of practice pads. A Gladstone pad fits over the drumhead so that the drum is not as loud. It is made of rubber and has a raised section in the middle that has much the same feel as a drumhead. A Gladstone pad can also be laid on a table for quieter practice.

Many practice pads consist of a thin rubber pad that is glued onto a wooden base. These are very portable and are usually the quietest pads.

Tunable practice pads consist of an actual drumhead that is mounted on a plastic or metal frame. They are louder than rubber pads, but they are still much quieter than practicing on a drum.

METRONOME

A metronome is a mechanical or electronic device that produces clicks or beeps that can be set to a specific tempo. Practicing with a metronome is very helpful because it helps you get a feel for playing in perfect time.

EAR PROTECTION

Drums and other percussion instruments are very loud, and if your ears are exposed to loud sounds on a frequent basis you can eventually suffer hearing damage. The first sign of potential ear damage is a ringing in the ears. At first, the ringing will usually go away after a couple of hours, but eventually it will be permanent.

Therefore, you should wear headphones or use earplugs when you are going to be exposed to loud music. Many drummers suffer the greatest damage as a result of practicing on a drum in a small room, so when you practice at home, either use a practice pad or wear hearing protection. When practicing or performing with a band, most drummers prefer foam earplugs that cannot be seen.

NOTATION

Music is written on a five-line staff that is divided into measures through the use of barlines. (A measure can also be referred to as a bar.)

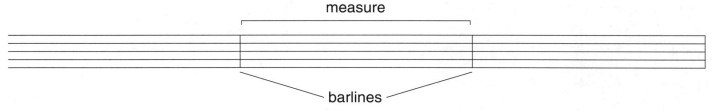

At the beginning of the staff you will see a clef sign. Most clef signs, such as treble clef or bass clef, are used to designate the pitches that are assigned to each line and space. Drum music, however, typically uses rhythm clef (sometimes called neutral clef), which indicates that the lines and spaces do not represent specific pitches. Occasionally, especially in older music, drum parts are written in bass clef.

Following the clef sign is a time signature. The top number tells you how many beats are in a measure. The bottom number tells you what type of note receives one beat.

$\frac{4}{4}$ four beats per measure $\frac{3}{4}$ three beats per measure $\frac{6}{8}$ six beats per measure
a quarter note gets one beat   a quarter note gets one beat   an eighth note gets one beat

Snare drum music is typically written on the third space of a standard five-line staff. A bass drum part may be notated on the first space.

COUNTING

Drumming is all about rhythm, which is all about counting. Therefore, you should always count when playing snare drum. In addition to counting the notes you are playing, it is also important to count the rests and any spaces between the notes.

Many of the exercises in this book include a suggested counting method. The number (or a subdivision such as "&") is shown above each note and rest. A number in parenthesis indicates a beat or subdivision that should be counted, although it might not be visible in the music because it is contained within a longer note.

STICKING

Two methods of sticking are typically used in snare drum playing. One method, known as right-hand lead or the "Straight system" (after Edward B. Straight, who invented it), uses right hand for the strong beats in a measure and left hand for the weaker beats. Many feel that this method is more consistent, because a specific rhythm is played the same way every time. This method is typically used in concert band and orchestra playing.

The other system is alternating sticking, in which the hands simply alternate between right and left. Some feel that this method is better for developing each hand equally and is more flexible. This style is typically used in marching band and rudimental-style drumming.

In this book, many examples show both styles of sticking, with right-hand lead directly under the music and alternating sticking underneath that. Use whichever method your drum teacher or band director recommends.

LESSON 1: QUARTER NOTES AND QUARTER RESTS

The 4/4 time signature indicates that each measure must contain four beats, and that a quarter note (♩) or a quarter rest (𝄽) receives one beat. Count as shown in each exercise, and use one of the sticking methods indicated below the music (R = right hand, L = left hand). Be sure to count the rests as well as the notes, and strive to make each note sound exactly the same.

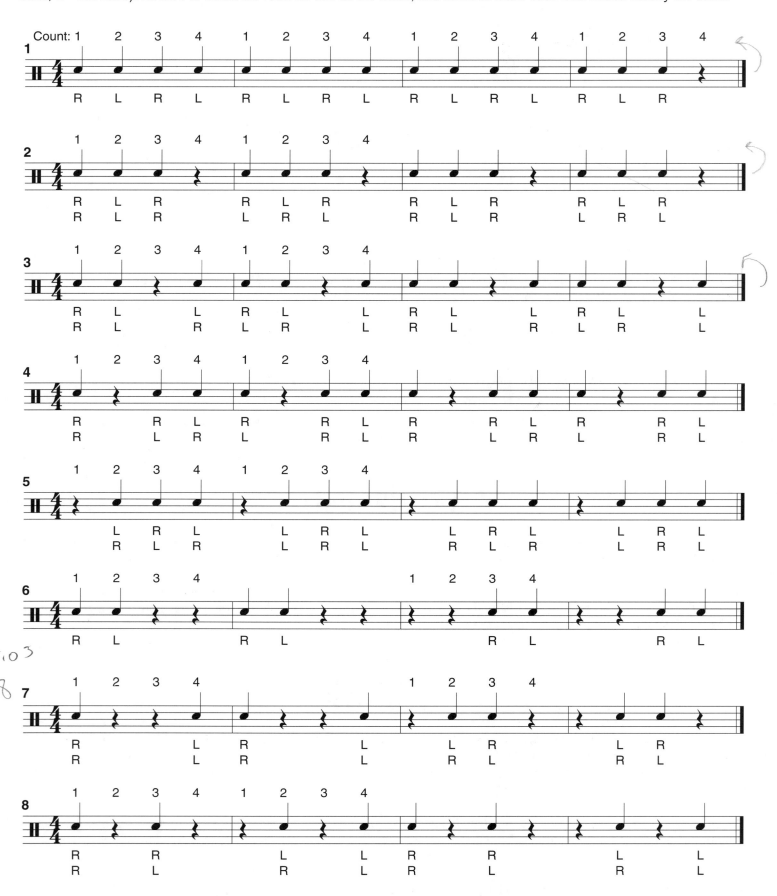

2.15.03
7-8

LESSON 2: HALF NOTES AND WHOLE NOTES

A half note is worth two beats in 4/4 time, which means it takes up twice as much space in a measure as a quarter note. A whole note takes up four beats, so it is equal to four quarter notes or two half notes.

In the examples below, the numbers in parenthesis ( ) represent beats that are contained within the previous note. These beats must be counted so that the notes receive their full value.

Repeat Sign

At the end of each exercise on this page you'll see two dots followed by a double bar. That is called a repeat sign, and it means to play the entire exercise again.

SOLO 1

The following snare drum solo uses the three types of notes you have learned so far: quarter notes, half notes, and whole notes. Count carefully and apply one of the sticking methods from Lesson 1.

Notice that instead of a 4/4 time signature at the beginning of the piece there is, instead, a **C**. This stands for **common time**, and is the same as 4/4 time.

You can listen to this solo, and then play along with it, on the accompanying CD. A click track, or metronome, is used to help you keep steady time. Before the solo begins, you will hear four clicks that will give you the tempo, or speed, of the solo.

2.15.03

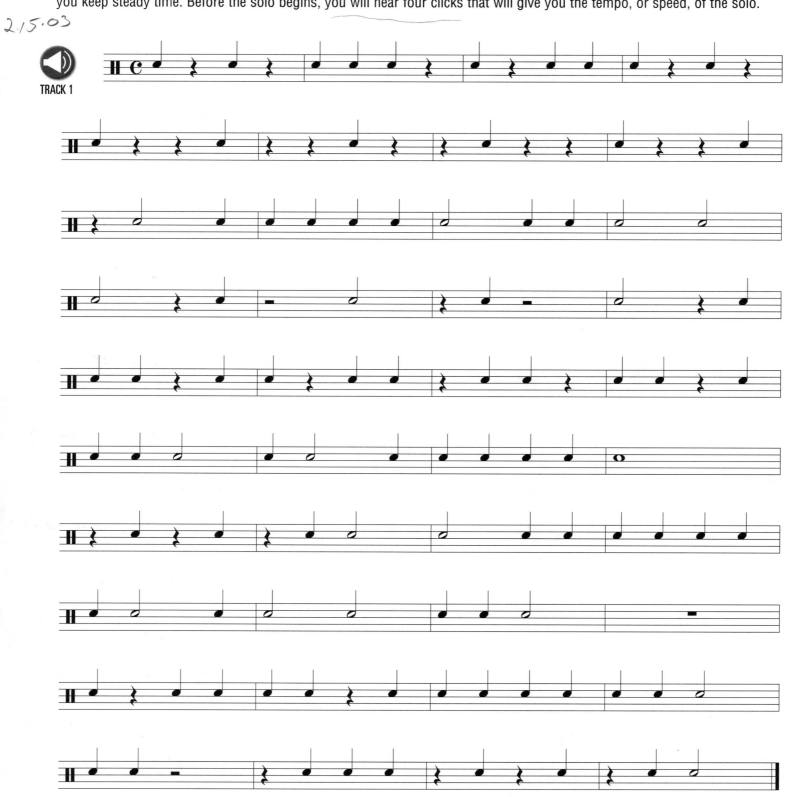

TRACK 1

LESSON 3:
INTRODUCTION TO MULTIPLE-BOUNCE STROKES

On a snare drum, quarter notes, half notes and whole notes all sound the same (except for how much time passes before the next note). Other musical instruments, however, can make the sound of a half note last twice as long as a quarter note, and the sound of a whole note last four times as long as a quarter note.

A snare drummer can make a note sound longer by playing a roll: many notes played very close together so that they resemble a continuous sound. The first step in learning to roll is to master the multiple-bounce stroke.

A multiple-bounce stroke is indicated by a Z on the note's stem. To play a multiple-bounce stroke, throw the stick down with a snap of the wrist and let it bounce rapidly on the drumhead, producing a "buzz" sound. (A multiple-bounce roll is sometimes called a buzz roll.)

In order for the stick to bounce, no fingers can be touching it, except at the "pivot point" between the thumb and first finger. Let the other fingers drop slightly so that they do not interfer with the bounces. If the bounces are too far apart, press the stick into the drumhead more. If the bounces don't last very long, you may be pressing the stick into the drum with too much force.

Listen to CD track 2, which demonstrates Example 1. Be patient, as it takes a lot of practice to develop a good multiple bounce.

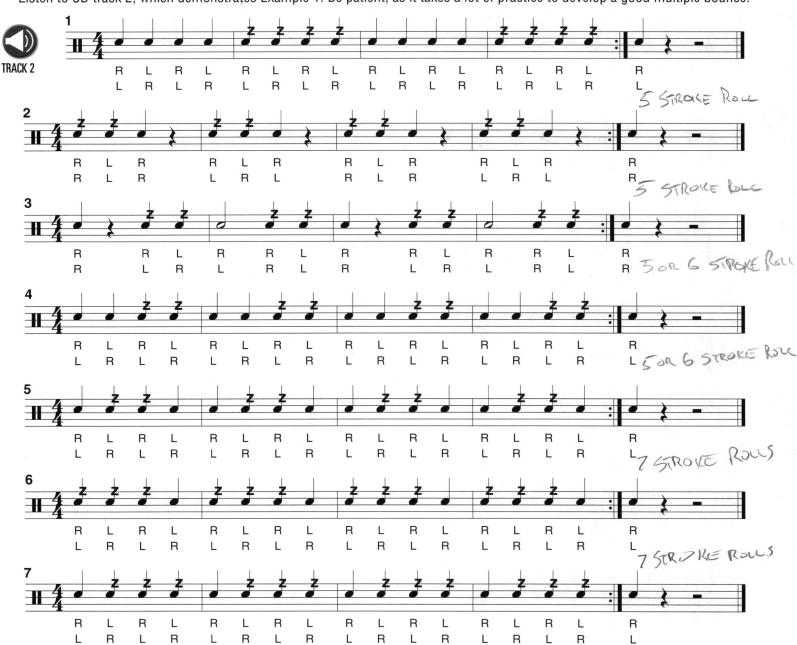

LESSON 4: EIGHTH NOTES

An eighth note is one-half the value of a quarter note. (Just like in math, 1/8 + 1/8 = 1/4.) In 4/4 time, since the quarter note gets the beat, we don't give each eighth note its own number. Instead, we count the note in-between the main beat as an "and" (&).

When mixing quarter notes and eighth notes, it is a good idea to count the & after each quarter note, so that you leave the appropriate amount of space after the note. In the exercises below, the &'s in parenthesis (&) indicate &'s that are counted but not played.

One eighth note by itself has a flag attached to its stem (♪).
Two or more eighth notes are often joined together by a single beam. ♪ ♪ = 🎵

SOLO 2

You can listen to this solo and play along with it on the accompanying CD. Before the solo begins, you will hear four metronome clicks that will give you the tempo of the quarter-note pulse.

TRACK 3

DUET 1

This duet is written for two snare drums — one with snares on and one with snares off. (The Snare Drum 2 part can also be played on a tom-tom.) The duet can be played by a student and teacher, or by two students.

On the accompanying CD, Track 4 contains both parts played together. Track 5 has just the Snare Drum 1 part, and Track 6 has only the Snare Drum 2 part. First, listen to Track 4 to see how the parts fit together. Then play along with Track 5 while you are working on the Snare Drum 1 part. Once you can play it with Track 5, try playing it along with Track 4.

After you are comfortable playing the Snare Drum 1 part with Track 5, play it with Track 6, which is just the Snare Drum 2 part. Listen to the Snare Drum 2 part carefully so that the two parts fit together well, but don't let the other part distract you from the part you are playing.

Repeat the process with the Snare Drum 2 part, first playing it along with Track 6, then playing it with Track 4, and finally playing it with Track 5.

Both parts
TRACK 4

Snare Drum 1 only
TRACK 5

Snare Drum 2 only
TRACK 6

FULL BAND PLAY-ALONG 1

Here is the Snare Drum/Bass Drum part that goes with the recording on Track 7 of the CD. You will hear four "clicks" at the beginning of the track, which will give you the tempo of the quarter notes. The word Moderato over the first measure indicates that the piece is played at a medium tempo.

Several measures consist of whole-note rests. Count very carefully during these measures so you don't lose your place. The last bar of the piece has a whole note with a multiple-bounce indication, and above it is a fermata sign, which is also called a "hold." This indicates that the note will be played longer than its usual value. Play a series of alternating multiple-bounce strokes for the length of the note. Try to get a smooth, uninterrupted sound that resembles a continuous tone.

HIGH ADVENTURE

PERCUSSION 1
Snare Drum, Bass Drum

PAUL LAVENDER (ASCAP)

LESSON 5: EIGHTH RESTS

An eighth rest takes the place of a single eighth note. In some of the exercises below, the same rhythm is notated in different ways to prepare you for the variety of notational styles you may encounter in different pieces of music.

LESSON 6: FLAMS

A flam is one of the basic rudiments of drumming. It consists of two notes that are played nearly at the same time. The sound should imitate the word "flam" and sound like one "fat" note — not two separate notes.

The small note is called a "grace note" and should be softer than the main note. It should also be played just before the main note so that the main note is played exactly on the beat. Flams are identified according to the main note: for a right-hand flam, the left hand plays the grace note and the right hand plays the main note; for a left-hand flam, the right hand plays the grace note and the left hand plays the main note.

Hand position is very important in playing flams. The hand that will play the grace note should only be about two inches above the drumhead; the hand that plays the main note should be higher. Once your hands are in the proper starting position, let them drop together as though both sticks are going to hit the drum at the same time. The stick that is closer to the drum will actually hit first, and it will also make a softer sound.

As the right hand strikes the drum, let the left stick return to full playing position. After the right hand strikes, let it rest about two inches above the drumhead. You are now in position for a left-hand flam. Reverse the process for a left-hand flam.

Starting position for a right-hand flam.

Starting position for a left-hand flam.

Practice the following exercises slowly, checking your hand positions carefully before each flam. Exercise 4 is demonstrated on CD track 8 so that you can hear how flams should sound.

SOLO 3

You can listen to this solo and play along with it on the accompanying CD. Before the solo begins, you will hear four metronome clicks that will give you the tempo of the quarter-note pulse.

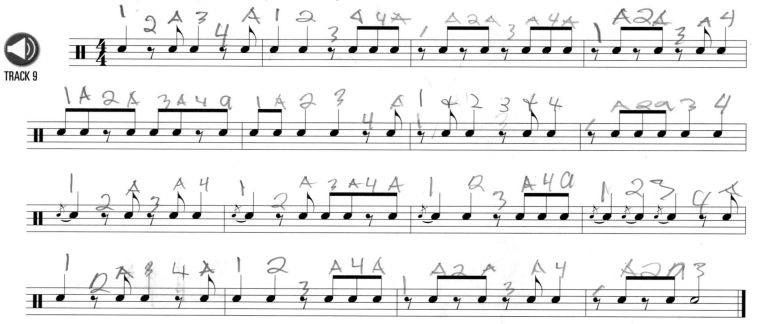

TRACK 9

DUET 2

This duet is written for two snare drums — one with snares on and one with snares off. (The Snare Drum 2 part can also be played on a tom-tom.) The duet can be played by a student and teacher, or by two students.

On the accompanying CD, Track 10 contains both parts played together. Track 11 has just the Snare Drum 1 part, and Track 12 has only the Snare Drum 2 part. First, listen to Track 10 to see how the parts fit together. You can use Track 11 to help you learn the Snare Drum 1 part, and you can use Track 12 to help you learn the Snare Drum 2 part.

Once you are comfortable with a part, you can practice it in duet style by playing it along with the CD track that has the other part.

Both parts

TRACK 10

Snare Drum 1 only

TRACK 11

Snare Drum 2 only

TRACK 12

LESSON 7: DOUBLE STROKES

Some drum rhythms require double strokes: two notes played with the same hand. Double strokes are used to play rolls, paradiddles, ruffs, and other common rudiments. Double strokes can also come in handy when you are using more than one drum, such as in a multi-tom setup or a drumset.

The following exercises will help you develop the ability to play double strokes. Try to make every note sound exactly the same. Do not play a "stroke and a bounce." A good double stroke consists of two even strokes. Later, when you start playing double strokes at faster tempos, you'll learn to use a "rebound stroke" for the second note, but for now, play two full wrist strokes.

PARADIDDLES

In rudimental terminology, a "diddle" is a double stroke. The Single Paradiddle rudiment consists of two single strokes and one double stroke. Single paradiddles are often played in pairs with the sticking R L R R L R L L, as shown in the example below.

Note: A true single paradiddle has an accent on the first note of each four-note group, which means you play that note a little bit louder. But for now, concentrate on learning the sticking pattern and making every note sound the same.

LESSON 8: DYNAMICS

The word "dynamics" refers to how loud or soft you are playing. Abbreviations for Italian words are used to indicate dynamics in music. The letter *p* stands for *piano*, which means soft. An *f* stands for *forte*, which means "loud." An *m* stands for *mezzo*, which means "medium"; therefore, *mp* (*mezzo piano*) is "medium soft" and *mf* (*mezzo forte*) is "medium loud." Sometimes you'll see such dynamics as *pp* or *fff*. The more *p*'s you have, the softer it is; the more *f*'s you have, the louder it is.

The following exercises use only *p*, *mf*, and *f*. Practice slowly at first and make sure you are playing at three distinct dynamic levels. Make the changes sudden when the dynamic changes; don't gradually get louder or softer.

DYNAMIC ETUDE

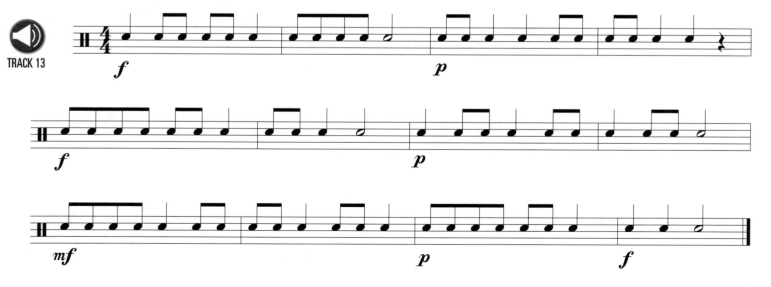

TRACK 13

LESSON 9: EIGHTH-NOTE MULTIPLE-BOUNCE STROKES

Get as many bounces as possible with each multiple-bounce stroke. When playing two or more multiple-bounce strokes in a row, strive to make the sound very even and each hand sound the same.

1

R L R R L R L R R L R etc.
R L R L R L R L R L R etc.

2

R L R L R R L R L R R etc.
R L R L R L R L R L R etc.

3

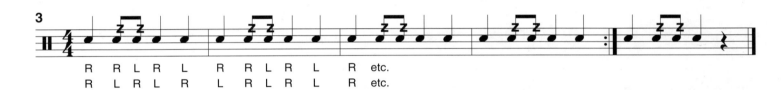

R R L R L R R L R L R etc.
R L R L R L R L R L R etc.

4

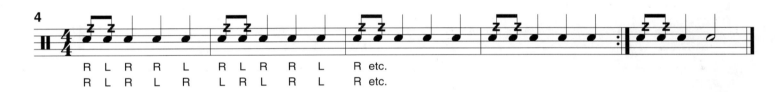

R L R R L R L R R L R etc.
R L R L R L R L R L R etc.

5

R R L R R L R R L R R L R etc.
R L R L R L R L R L R L R etc.

6

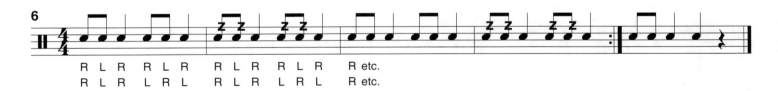

R L R R L R R L R R L R etc.
R L R L R L R L R L R L R etc.

7

R R L R L R R R L R L R R etc.
R L R L R L R L R L R L R etc.

TRACK 14

8

R L R L R L R L R L R L R L R L etc.
L R L R L R L R L R L R L R L R etc.

21

FULL BAND PLAY-ALONG 2

This is the Snare Drum/Bass Drum part that goes with the recording on CD Track 15. The four "clicks" at the beginning of the track give you the tempo of the quarter notes. Notice that the snares are to be released at the beginning of the piece, giving the drum a tom-tom sound. The snares are turned on before measure 33, and released again for the final two measures. Don't let the snares or the snare strainer make any noise when you are turning the snares off and on.

THE LOST CITY

PERCUSSION 1

Snare Drum, Bass Drum

PAUL LAVENDER (ASCAP)

LESSON 10: 2/4 TIME

A measure of 2/4 time is half as long as a measure of 4/4. In 2/4, the quarter note still gets the beat, but there are only two beats per measure. So the relative values of quarter notes, eighth notes, and half notes remains the same. (You can't have a whole note in 2/4 time because it takes up four beats.) You can use the same sticking method that you use in 4/4 time.

Pay particular attention to exercises 7 and 8 on this page. The rhythm sounds the same throughout each exercise, but measures two and four of each line are written with a quarter note on the & of beat 1. So instead of the quarter note being counted with a number and then an &, this time the & comes first, followed by the number. Putting a strong note on a weak beat in this manner is called **syncopation**.

2/4 ETUDE

Moderato

TRACK 16

2/4 DUET

Both parts
TRACK 17

Snare Drum 1 only
TRACK 18

Snare Drum 2 only
TRACK 19

Snare Drum 1
Snare Drum 2
(snares off)

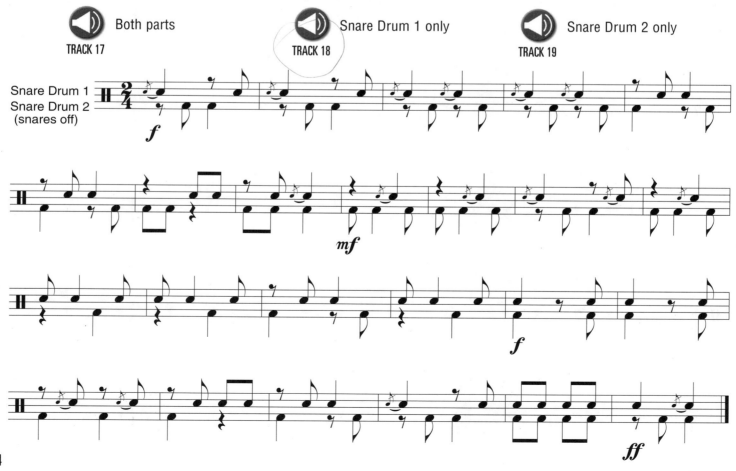

LESSON 11: FLAM TAP AND FLAM PARADIDDLE

It is sometimes said that all of the drum rudiments are combinations of three basic strokes: single strokes, double strokes, and flams. (You will find a chart with all of the major drum rudiments at the end of this book.)

The **Flam Tap** uses a combination of flams and double strokes:

The **Flam Paradiddle** consists of paradiddles (which are made up of single strokes and double strokes) with flams on the first note of each group. (Sometimes, a Flam Paradiddle is called a "Flamadiddle.")

FLAM RUDIMENT ETUDE

Pay very close attention to the sticking in the following solo. Play it slowly at first so that the flams are played cleanly.

LESSON 12: TIES + SLURS

When two notes are joined by a tie, do not play the second note. Think of the second note as a continuation of the first note. For example, a half note is being created by tying together two quarter notes.

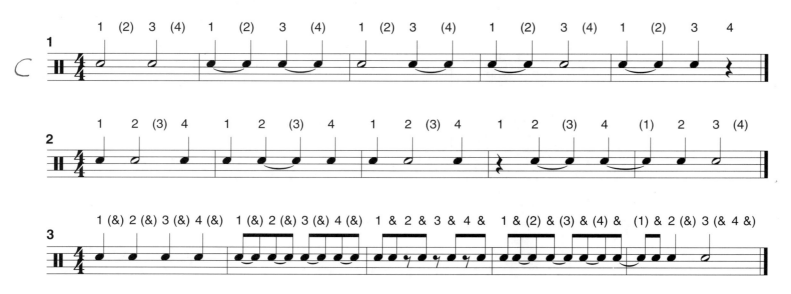

In drum music, when a note that is being rolled is tied to another note, the purpose is to show you exactly where the roll should end with a single stroke. So when a roll is involved, you do play both notes that are tied. In the examples below, you will first see how a particular measure is played, and then you will see how the same measure is usually written. Notice that through the use of ties, only the first and last note of a roll are shown.

If a roll is not tied, you have to end the roll before the next note is struck. The following examples will show you the difference between tied and non-tied half-note and whole-note rolls.

LESSON 13: REPEATS

ONE-BAR REPEATS
When the same measure is to be played more than once, a repeat symbol is often used. If there are several repeat measures in a row, some of them may be numbered in order to help you keep your place. But each repeat symbol represents only one measure of music.

TWO-BAR REPEATS
The symbol shown in the example below is a two-bar repeat. It does NOT mean to repeat the same measure twice, however. Rather, it means to repeat the two previous measures, as indicated below.

Repeat two bars one time each   Repeat one bar twice

SECTION REPEATS
A section of music that is within repeat bars is to be played twice. For example, in the illustration below, you would play measures 1 through 6, then repeat measures 3 through 6, and then play measures 7 and 8.

1.31.04

REPEATS ETUDE
The etude below has section repeats in measures 9–12 and 21–28. Notice that there are two dynamics shown in measure 21. The first time you play that section it should be played soft (p); when you repeat it, play it moderately loud (mf).

TRACK 21

LESSON 14: 3/4 TIME

In 3/4 time, there are three beats per measure and the quarter note gets one beat,. The relative values of quarter notes, eighth notes, and half notes remains the same as in 4/4 and 2/4.

Exercises 5 introduces the **dotted half note**. A dot increases a note's value by one-half. So, because a half note is worth two beats, a dotted half note is worth three beats. Therefore, a dotted half note takes up a full measure in 3/4 time.

2.22.04
15,6

2.22.04
DOUBLE PARADIDDLE

3/4 ETUDE

TRACK 22

3/4 DUET

The first four measures of this duet (as well as measures 9–12) sound as if they were written in 2/4, so you have to count very carefully. Pay close attention to the dynamics and make sure you are playing at the same volume level as the other part.

Both parts — **TRACK 23**

Snare Drum 1 only — **TRACK 24**

Snare Drum 2 only — **TRACK 25**

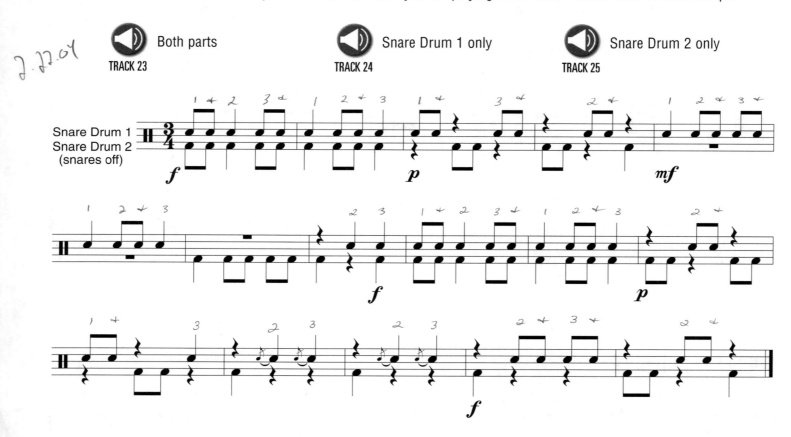

Snare Drum 1
Snare Drum 2
(snares off)

LESSON 15: ACCENTS

A note with an accent (>) is played a little bit louder. The loudness of an accented note depends on the dynamic marking. For example, if the dynamic is *mf*, the accented note is not as loud as an accented note in a section marked *f*:

ACCENT ETUDE

CRESCENDO AND DIMINUENDO

A crescendo (⟨ or *cresc.*) indicates that you should gradually get louder until you reach the next dynamic level that is indicated. A diminuendo (⟩ or *dim.*) means that each note should be a little softer than the one before until you reach the next dynamic mark. A diminuendo can also be called a decrescendo.

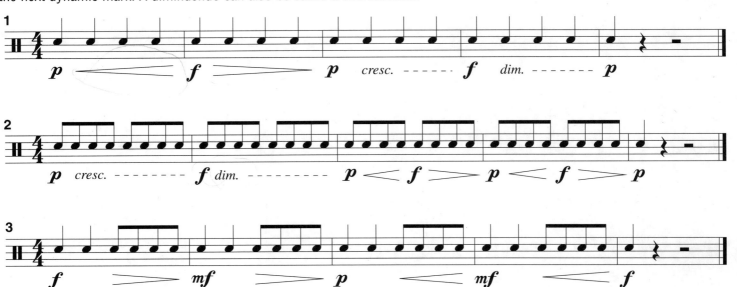

LESSON 16: 1ST AND 2ND ENDINGS

Sometimes a repeated section of music will have two (or more) different endings. Generally these endings are one or two measures each, but they can be longer. The endings are indicated by brackets over the music that look like this:

In the etude below, play the first ten measures and then play the 1st ending (measures 11 and 12). Take the repeat and play measures 5 through 10 again. This time, skip the 1st ending and play the 2nd ending (measures 13 and 14). Play measures 15 through 22 twice, as indicated by the repeat marks, then play measures 23 through 37, followed by the 1st ending (measure 38). Play measures 31 through 37 again, then skip the 1st ending and play the 2nd ending (measure 39).

REVIEW DUET

Snare Drum 1
Snare Drum 2
(snares off)

33

LESSON 17: SIXTEENTH NOTES

A sixteenth note is one-fourth the value of a quarter note and one-half the value of an eighth note. Just as we put an "&' in-between each number when we counted eighth notes, we will now put counts in-between the numbers and the &'s, so that the full count in 4/4 time is 1 e & a 2 e & a 3 e & a 4 e & a.

When mixing quarter notes, eighth notes, and sixteenth notes, it is a good idea to count all of the sixteenth subdivisions after each quarter note and in-between the eighth notes, so that you leave the appropriate amount of space after each note and maintain a steady tempo. In the exercises below, the e's, &'s, and a's in parenthesis indicate subdivisions that are counted but not played.

One sixteenth note by itself has a double flag attached to its stem (♪) and a sixteenth-note rest also has two flags (♪). Two, three, or four sixteenth notes are usually joined together by a double beam when they are part of the same beat.

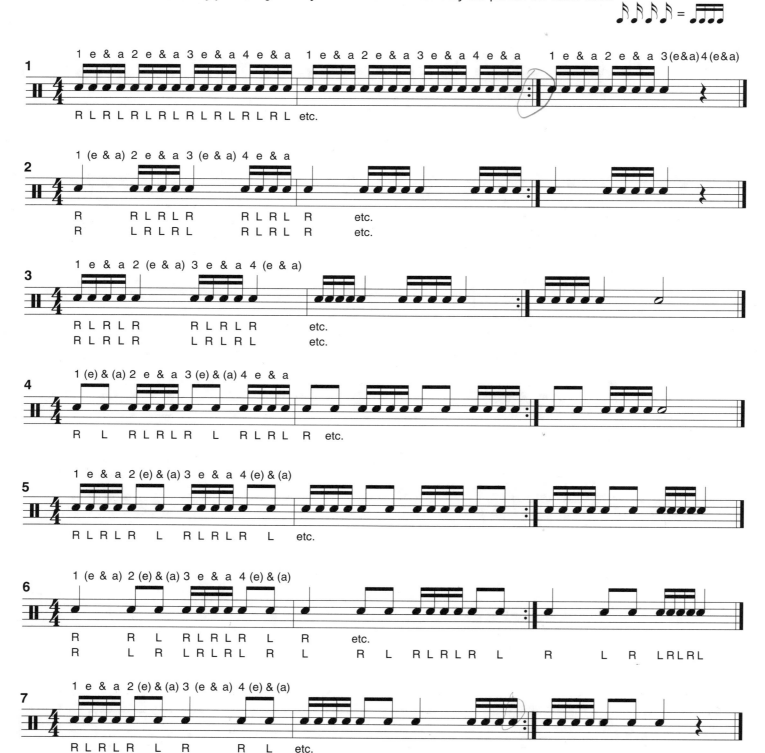

Several examples on this page show the same rhythm notated two different ways: with combinations of sixteenths and sixteenth rests, and with combinations of eighth and sixteenth notes. You are more likely to see the eighth/sixteenth combinations in actual music, but you must be able to recognize the rhythms no matter how they are notated.

ETUDE WITH SIXTEENTH NOTES

DUET WITH SIXTEENTH NOTES

At the very end of this duet you'll see the words **D.C. al Fine.** The **D.C.** stands for *da capo*, which means "go back to the beginning." *Fine* means "final" or "end," and you will notice that there is a *Fine* indication at the end of measure 8. Therefore, play this duet from beginning to end, then go back to the beginning and play measures 1 through 8 again.

Pay close attention to the dynamic marks in this duet and notice that each part has its own dynamics. It the first section, both parts are marked forte, and at the beginning of the second section (mesure 9), both parts drop to mezzo forte. But at measure 11, Snare Drum 1 drops to piano while Snare Drum 2 continues to play mf. Snare Drum 1 returns to mezzo forte in measure 12, and continues to play mf even when Snare Drum 2 drops to piano in measure 15.

Both parts
TRACK 31

Snare Drum 1 only
TRACK 32

Snare Drum 2 only
TRACK 33

LESSON 18: DOTTED NOTES

When a note or rest has a dot after it, the value of that note increases by half. As we saw in Lesson 14, a dotted half note is worth three beats. We can apply that same idea to other note values. A quarter note or quarter rest is worth one beat, so a dotted quarter is worth one and a half beats. An eighth note or eighth rest is worth one-half of a beat, so a dotted eighth is worth three-fourths of a beat. The chart below illustrates one way of understanding the value of various dotted notes.

Several of the exercises below show how the same rhythm can be written different ways using various combinations of notes, rests, ties, and dotted notes.

FULL BAND PLAY-ALONG 3

This is the snare drum part that goes with the recording on CD Track 34. Four clicks at the beginning will give you the tempo of the quarter-note pulse. There are many repeated measures in this part, which is typical of snare drum parts. Count very carefully so you don't lose your place.

LATIN FIRE

SNARE DRUM

JOHN HIGGINS (ASCAP)

LESSON 19: 5-STROKE ROLLS

We will now apply multiple-bounce (or buzz) strokes to sixteenth-note rhythms and use actual roll notation. We will start with the 5-stroke roll. This terminology comes from the rudimental style of drumming in which double strokes are used instead of buzz strokes. In the rudimental style, the 5-stroke roll consists of two double strokes and a single stroke. In "orchestral" style, a 5-stroke roll consists of two buzz strokes and a single stroke.

Rudimental Style: Double Strokes

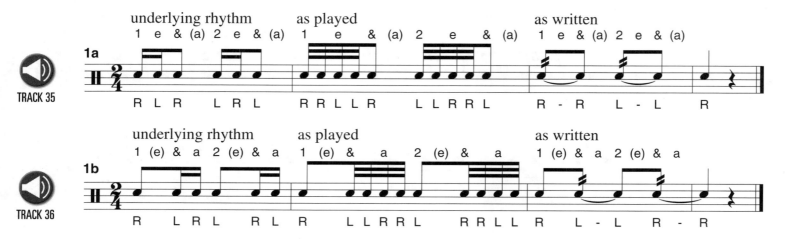

Orchestral Style: Buzz Strokes

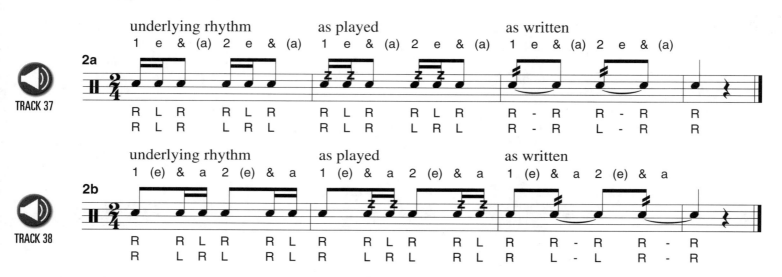

The following etude can be played using either double-stroke rolls or buzz rolls.

LESSON 20: 9-STROKE AND 17-STROKE ROLLS

9-STROKE ROLLS

Rudimental Style: Double Strokes

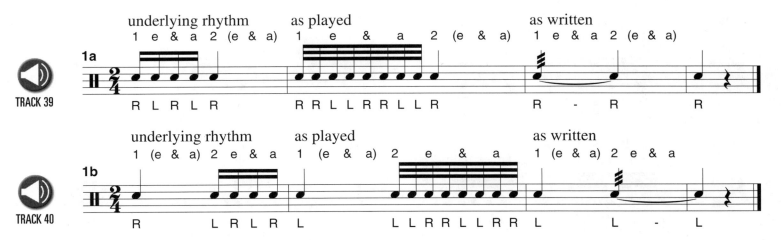

TRACK 39

TRACK 40

Orchestral Style: Buzz Strokes

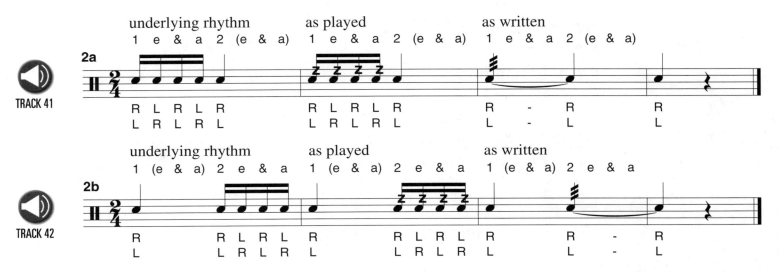

TRACK 41

TRACK 42

17-STROKE ROLLS

Rudimental Style: Double Strokes

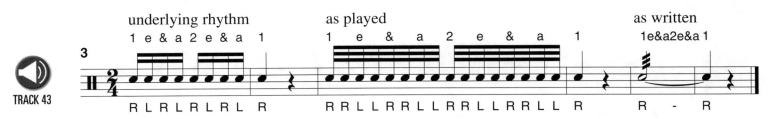

TRACK 43

Orchestral Style: Buzz Strokes

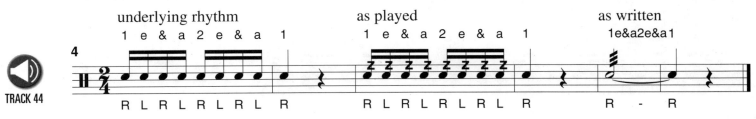

TRACK 44

LESSON 21: ACCENTED ROLLS

When a roll has an accent over the first note, accent only the first note and play the rest of the roll at the regular dynamic level. The last note of a roll can also be accented. Be sure that only the final note is louder; do not crescendo up to the accent. The following chart shows how to play different accented rolls both rudimentally (with double strokes) and orchestrally (with buzz strokes).

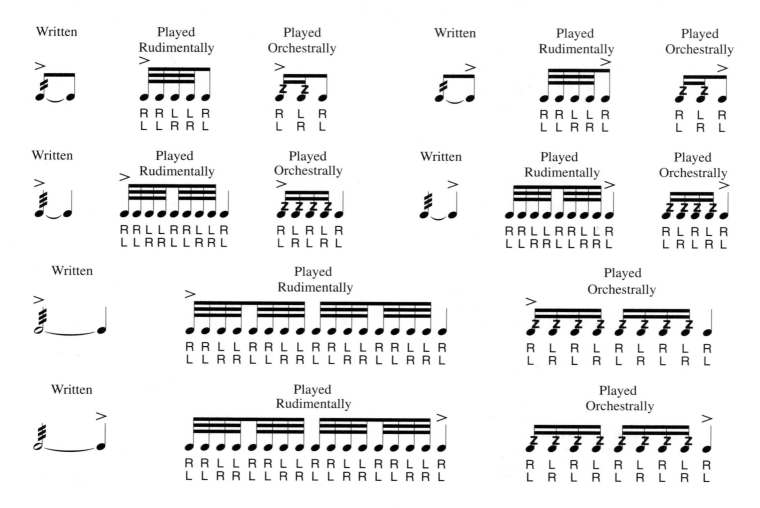

ACCENTED ROLL ETUDE

This solo can be played with either rudimental or orchestral rolls. The four-bar pattern that begins this etude is called a **roll-off**.

FULL BAND PLAY-ALONG 4

The last measure of this part is marked *D.C. al Fine*, which means to go back to the beginning and play until the *Fine* sign. But when you are taking the *D.C.* and repeating a section that has 1st and 2nd endings, skip the 1st ending and go straight to the 2nd ending.

This drum part also includes multi-measure rests. These are used to indicate two or more measures in which you do not play.

A good way to keep your place during multi-measure rests is to count the measure number at the beginning of each bar. For example, during the four-bar multi-measure rest near the end of this piece, you might count "1 & 2 &, 2 & 2 &, 3 & 2 &, 4 & 2 &. (You don't have to count every sixteenth subdivision when counting rests.)

AMERICAN SPIRIT MARCH

SNARE DRUM

JOHN HIGGINS (ASCAP)

LESSON 22: CUT TIME

In Solo 1 you saw that another way to indicate 4/4 time was with a $\mathbf{C}$, which stands for common time. If the symbol has a vertical slash ($\mathbf{\mathcal{C}}$), it stands for **cut time**. In cut time, every note value is cut in half, which means that a quarter note gets half a beat instead of a full beat. An eighth note in cut time gets one-fourth of a beat. In other words, in cut time a quarter note is counted like an eighth note in 4/4, and a cut-time eighth note is counted like a sixteenth note in 4/4.

Just as common time ($\mathbf{C}$) is the same as 4/4, cut time ($\mathbf{\mathcal{C}}$) is the same as 2/2. In 2/2 time, there are two beats per measure and the half note gets one beat. Therefore, just as in cut time, a quarter note gets half a beat and an eighth note gets one-fourth of a beat.

LESSON 23: CUT-TIME ROLLS

The following chart shows how different cut-time rolls are written and how they are played using buzz strokes. For the rudimental style, substitute a double stroke for each buzz stroke.

In each of the following exercises, cut-time rolls are shown first as they are played and counted, and then as they are written.

CUT-TIME ETUDE

FULL BAND PLAY-ALONG 5

This piece employs playing on the rim in measures 9–16 and 76–75 to give the snare drum part a different "color."

PARADE OF THE WOODEN SOLDIERS

PERCUSSION 1

Snare Drum, Bass Drum

Music by LEON JESSEL
Arranged by PAUL LAVENDER

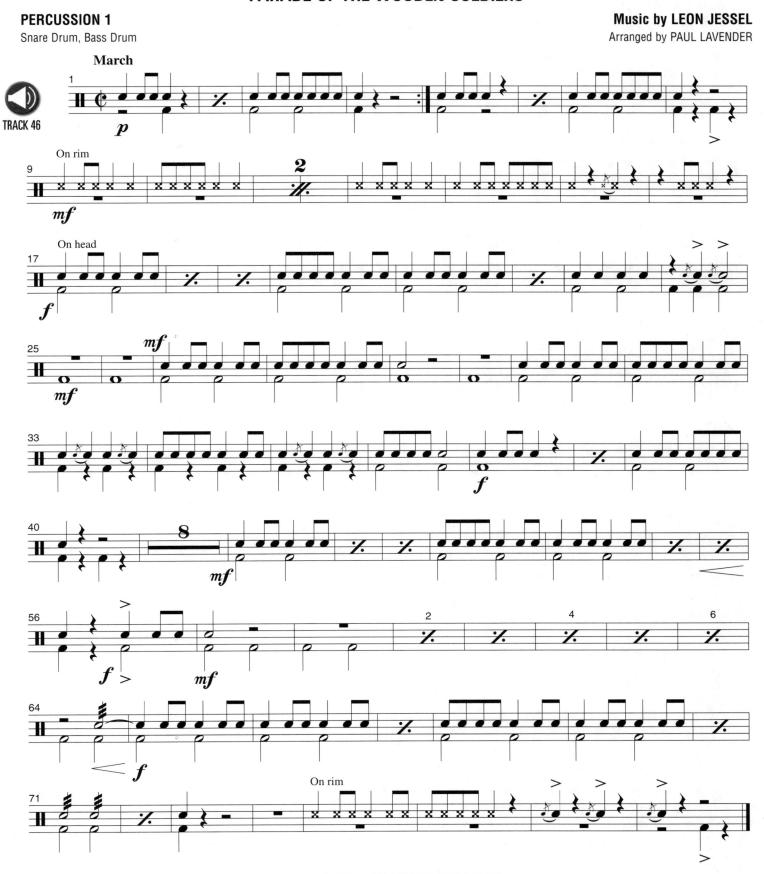

LESSON 24: 6/8 TIME

We will now count eighth-note beats instead of quarter-note beats. In 6/8 time, there are six eighth notes — or combinations of note values that add up to six eighth notes.

In medium or slow tempos, 6/8 is counted "in six," with each eighth note getting a number (1 2 3 4 5 6) or count. A quarter note gets two numbers or counts; a dotted quarter note gets three numbers or counts.

In faster tempos, 6/8 is often counted "in two" (1 & a 2 & a). In the first three exercises below, both ways of counting are shown. Start slowly, counting in six. When you are comfortable with the patterns, increase the tempo and count in two.

ETUDE

LESSON 25: 6/8 WITH ACCENTS

ACCENT ETUDE

LESSON 26: 6/8 WITH FLAMS

FULL BAND PLAY-ALONG 6

This excerpt from a famous march begins with a single eighth-note (the rest of the band actually plays the note, but for the snare drum it's a rest). Any introductory notes played before the first measure of music are called **pickup notes**. This march is played "in two," so on CD track 47 you will hear two clicks, which will give you the tempo of the dotted-quarter-note pulse.

LIBERTY BELL MARCH (EXCERPT)

SNARE DRUM

JOHN PHILIP SOUSA
Arranged by PAUL LAVENDER

TRACK 47

6/8 DUET

The *sfz* over the final note of this duet stands for *sforzando*, which is a very strong accent.

Both parts
TRACK 48

Snare Drum 1 only
TRACK 49

Snare Drum 2 only
TRACK 50

LESSON 27: 6/8 WITH SIXTEENTHS

In 6/8 time, a sixteenth note or rest gets one-half a beat. When we are counting in six, the sixteenth notes in-between the numbers are counted with &'s. But when 6/8 is being counted in two, we don't typically use numbers, syllables or letters for the sixteenth notes that are in-between the 1 & a 2 a & counts. Just place those notes evenly between the notes you are counting.

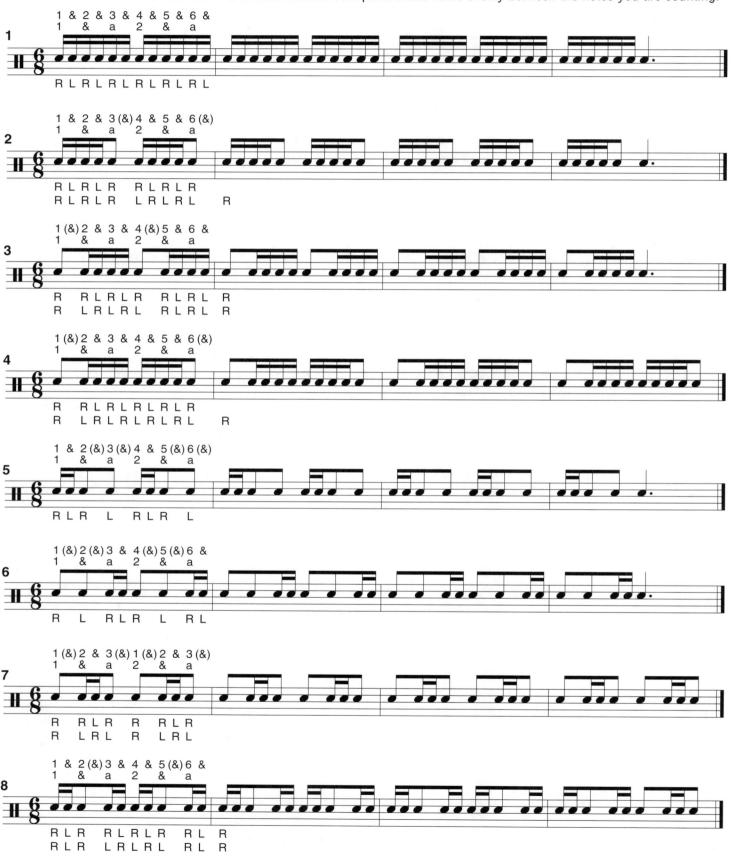

LESSON 28: 6/8 ROLLS

The following examples show how rolls are played in slower tempos when 6/8 is being counted in six. (The &'s are not shown between the numbers, but you can count them if you like.) These rolls are notated only in orchestral style. For rudimental style, substitute a double stroke for each multiple-bounce stroke.

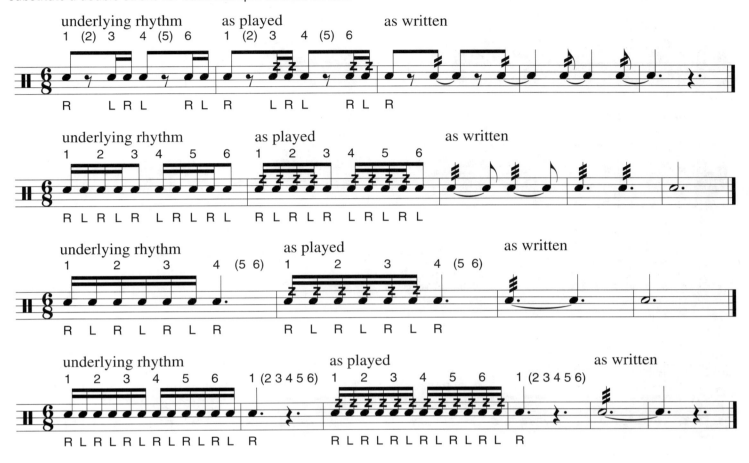

Here are some typical 6/8 phrases using rolls. Count these in six.

At faster tempos, when 6/8 is being counted in two, you won't have time to play rolls as buzzed sixteenth notes, so you will have to simply play eighth notes with multiple-bounce strokes. The examples below illustrate the most typical patterns. These rolls are notated only in orchestral style. For rudimental style, substitute a double stroke for each multiple-bounce stroke. (In these rolls, the double strokes will be sixteenth notes.)

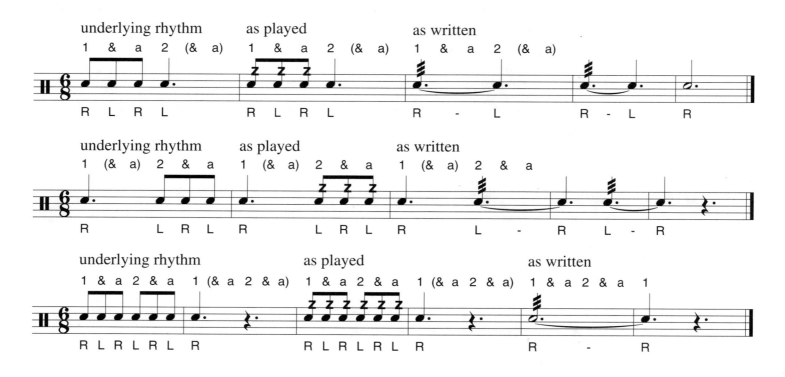

Here are some typical 6/8 phrases using rolls. Count these in two.

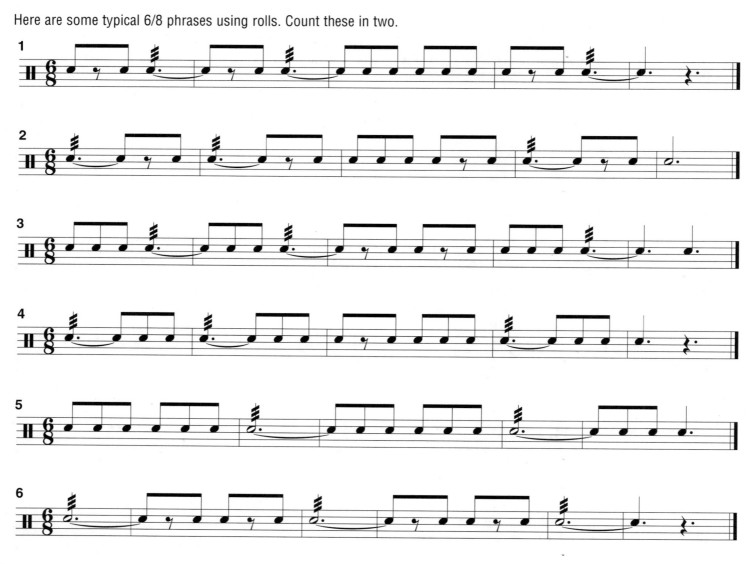

LESSON 29: THE DRAG RUDIMENT

The drag (which is also known as a 3-stroke ruff) consists of two grace notes followed by a main note. Like the flam, the main note is played on the beat and the grace notes are played just before the main note. Also, like the flam, the grace notes are played a little softer than the main note.

In most situations, the grace notes should be played as a double stroke. Sometimes at very fast tempos in orchestral or concert style drumming, the grace notes in a drag are played as a very short multiple-bounce stroke.

The drag is one of the basic rudiments of drumming, and several other rudiments are based on the drag stroke. Two of them, the Single Drag Tap and the Double Drag Tap, are shown below. For a complete list of the drag rudiments, see page 63.

ETUDE

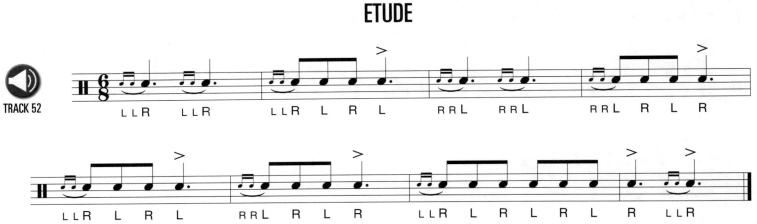

55

FULL BAND PLAY-ALONG 7

Snare drum parts are sometimes written on a single-line staff, as in this example from a famous march.

SEMPRE FIDELES

SNARE DRUM

JOHN PHILIP SOUSA
Arranged by PAUL LAVENDER

TRACK 53

LESSON 30: EIGHTH-NOTE TRIPLETS

A triplet consists of three notes played in the space of two notes. An eighth-note triplet, therefore, consists of three eighth notes played in the space of two eighth notes. In other words, whereas regular eighth notes divide a quarter note into halves, triplet eighth notes divide a quarter note into thirds. Triplets are always indicated with a number 3.

Straight eighth-note triplets, such as the ones shown in Exercise 1 below, are sometimes counted "1 & a 2 & a 3 & a 4 & a." However, this can be confused with "1 (e) & a 2 (e) & a ..." and result in uneven triplets. Also, that method of counting is difficult to apply to sixteenth-note triplets.

Another way of counting triplets is to use the regular beat number for the first note of the triplet, the syllable "trip" for the second note, and the syllable "let" for the third note. In the examples below, "trip" is represented by a T and "let" by an L.

To get the feel of triplets, count straight triplets throughout the following exercises, as indicated. You can also play along with selected exercises that are included on the CD that accompanies this book. Once you are comfortable with the triplet feel, try playing the exercises just counting the quarter-note pulse (1 2 3 4) and feeling the triplet subdivisions within the beats.

LESSON 31:
EIGHTH NOTES AND EIGHTH-NOTE TRIPLETS

When mixing eighth-note triplets with regular eighth notes, the best way to ensure a consistent tempo and rhythmic accuracy is to concentrate on the quarter-note pulse. In other words, just count the main beats (1 2 3 4) and feel the subdivisions in halves (eighth notes) or thirds (eighth-note triplets). Playing along with the exercises on this page that are recorded on the CD will help you get the feel of the subdivisions. Tapping your foot on the main beats (quarter-note pulse) will help you keep a steady tempo and also help develop coordination between your hands and feet.

ETUDE

LESSON 32: SIXTEENTH-NOTE TRIPLETS

A sixteenth-note triplet consists of three sixteenth notes played in the space of two sixteenth notes. Whereas regular sixteenth notes divide an eighth note into halves, triplet sixteenth notes divide an eighth note into thirds.

When counting sixteenth-note triplets, we will use the regular numbers and &'s for the eighth-note pulse and continue to use the syllable "trip" for the second note of the triplet and the syllable "let" for the third note. In the examples below, "trip" is represented by a T and "let" by an L. Once you are comfortable with the triplet feel, try playing the following exercises just counting the eighth-note pulse (1 & 2 &) and feeling the triplet subdivisions within the beats.

LESSON 33: TRIPLET ROLLS

How a roll is played depends on the tempo of the music. Look at the following example, which contains quarter-note and half-note rolls.

At a slow tempo, the rolls would be played as multiple-bounce sixteenth notes:

TRACK 62

At a fast tempo, the rolls would be played as multiple-bounce eighth notes:

TRACK 63

At a medium tempo, you might have trouble squeezing in multiple-bounce sixteenth notes, but if you only play multiple-bounce eighth notes, they may be too far apart and the roll will not be a continuous sound. In such a situation, you can think of the rolls as multiple-bounce triplets:

TRACK 64

The following exercises will help you develop the ability to play triplet rolls.

FULL BAND PLAY-ALONG 8

This part from a popular ballet score includes cue notes, which are small notes that indicate another instrument's part. Cue notes are used to help you keep your place in the music when your part has several bars in a row during which you do not play. In this part, there is a cymbal cue in measure 24 and a xylophone cue in measures 26–32. In addition, there is a word cue (with Tpts) above measure 9, which tells you that the trumpets begin playing in that measure, and that the snare drum part should blend rhythmically with the trumpet part.

ELVES' DANCE
From The Nutcracker

SNARE DRUM

PETER I. TCHAIKOVSKY
Arranged by PAUL LAVENDER

PERCUSSIVE ARTS SOCIETY INERNATIONAL DRUM RUDIMENTS

All rudiments should be practiced: open (slow) to close (fast) to open (slow) and/or at an even moderate march tempo.

I. ROLL RUDIMENTS

A. Single Stroke Roll Rudiments

1. Single Stroke Roll*

R L R L R L R L

2. Single Stroke Four

R L R L   R L R L
L R L R   L R L R

3. Single Stroke Seven
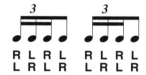
R L R L R L R
L R L R L R L

B. Multiple Bounce Roll Rudiments

4. Multiple Bounce Roll

5. Triple Stroke Roll

R R R L L L R R R L L L

C. Double Stroke Open Roll Rudiments

6. Double Stroke Open Roll*

R R L L R R L L

7. Five Stroke Roll*

R   R   L   L

8. Six Stroke Roll
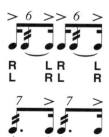
R   L R   L
L   R L   R

9. Seven Stroke Roll*
R   L R   L
L   R L   R

10. Nine Stroke Roll*

R   R   L   L

11. Ten Stroke Roll*

R   R L   R   R L

12. Eleven Stroke Roll*

R   R L   R   R L

13. Thirteen Stroke Roll*
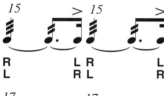
R   R L   L

14. Fifteen Stroke Roll*

R   L R   L
L   R L   R

15. Seventeen Stroke Roll

R   R L   L

II. DIDDLE RUDIMENTS

16. Single Paradiddle*

R L R R L R L L

17. Double Paradiddle*

R L R L R R L R L R L L

18. Triple Paradiddle
R L R L R L R R L R L R L R L L

18. Single Paradiddle-Diddle
R L R R L L R L R R L L
L R L L R R L R L L R R

www.pas.org

III. FLAM RUDIMENTS

20. Flam*

22. Flam Accent*

22. Flam Tap*

23. Flamacue*

24. Flam Paradiddle*

25. Single Flammed Mill

26. Flam Paradiddle-Diddle

27. Pataflafla

28. Swiss Army Triplet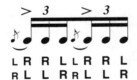

29. Inverted Flam Tap

30. Flam Drag

IV. DRAG RUDIMENTS

31. Drag*

32. Single Drag Tap*

33. Double Drag Tap*

34. Lesson 25*

35. Single Dragadiddle

36. Drag Paradiddle #1*

37. Drag Paradiddle #2*

38. Single Ratamacue*

39. Double Ratamacue*

40. Triple Ratamacue*

For information on becoming a member of the Percussive Arts Society™ contact PAS® at:
701 N.W. Ferris Ave., Lawton, OK 73507 • (580) 353-1456 • E-mail: percarts@pas.org • Web site: www.pas.org